Paleo Recipes for Kids

---

50 Delicious Paleo

Recipes Your Kids Will

Love You For!

By: Natalie Ray

Disclaimer

The author of this book is not affiliated with any medical company, nor does the author provide medical treatment advice in any way. The ideas, views, and opinions expressed in this book are those of the author. The author assumes no liability for advice or suggestions offered in this book. The author and publisher of this book and the accompanying materials have used their best efforts in preparing this book. The author and publisher make no representation or warranties with respect to the accuracy, applicability, fitness, or completeness of the contents of this book. The information contained in this book is strictly for informational purposes. Therefore, if you wish to apply ideas contained in this book, you are taking full responsibility for your actions.

Table of Contents

Introduction

Most adults don't like the word diet, let alone apply it to the children in their house. However, many people look at a diet as being a strict way to eat food, when in reality, it is not. A diet simply means what foods and beverages a person consumes on a regular basis. Having a family on a particular diet might actually be a very good thing for you.

A Paleo Diet is a good thing to start a child on early. Why? Because it focuses on only eating the foods that are good for you like fruits, meats and vegetables that are available in their natural form.

The Paleo Diet originates from how the cavemen ate. If they wouldn't have eaten the food or been able to prepare it, then it isn't consumed. Following the Paleo Diet eliminates all of the processed foods, dairy products and other sauces that are high in fat, calories and sodium and aren't good for you anyway.

Starting your kids on a Paleo Diet might not be hard at all. If they naturally love fruits and vegetables, then you are most of the way there. If not, then this eBook is a way to get started in transitioning them in to eating Paleo friendly foods so they have a healthier lifestyle.

Chapter 1: Breakfast Recipes

Breakfast is the most important meal of the day, especially when the kids are going off to school. They need protein to help them think better and function at school at an optimum level. Luckily there are lots of breakfast recipes that kids will love to eat, whether it is before school or on the weekend.

Paleo Pancakes

This pancake recipe utilizes the sweetness of sweet potatoes to make them irresistible.

Ingredients:

1 large sweet potato
2 eggs
½ banana
1/4 tsp baking soda
Pinch of Salt, Cinnamon, Nutmeg, and Ginger

Poke the potato with a fork and microwave for five minutes or until soft. Scoop out the insides and place in to a food processor. Pulse and then add the eggs and banana. Mix until smooth. Add the rest of the **Ingredients** and mix.

Heat a skillet and scoop small amounts of batter to fry pancakes. Cook on one side for 3 minutes and flip. Cook until the batter is done.

Fruit Kabobs

These kabobs can be made several days ahead of time and stored in a container so the kids can grab one out whenever they want, whether it is breakfast or not.

Ingredients:

Strawberry chunks
Blueberries
Blackberries
Melon pieces
Bamboo skewers

Cut up chunks of desired fruit the kids like. Cut it in to chunks or fun shapes using a cookie cutter. String along wood skewer and serve for breakfast.

Crepes

Crepes might just look like skinny pancakes, but they really do have a different taste to them. This recipe includes hazelnut topping for added flavor.

Ingredients:
3 eggs
1 tbsp vanilla
2 tbsp coconut flour
½ cup coconut milk

Mix all of the **Ingredients** together with a whisk.

On a hot skillet, pour batter in small circles and cook until bubbly on one side. Flip and cook for an additional minute or two. Cover with hazelnut spread below.

Ingredients:

1 cup unsalted hazelnuts
3 oz bittersweet chocolate
2 tbsp extra virgin coconut oil

Grind the hazelnuts in a food processor.

In a saucepan, melt the chocolate and oil. Remove from the heat and stir in hazelnut paste. Mix well. Spread over prepared crepes.

French Toast

This French toast recipe is great for a lazy family breakfast – if you ever get the chance to have one!

Ingredients:

8 eggs
¼ cup maple syrup
1 ½ tbsp cinnamon
1/3 cup coconut flour
1/3 cup coconut milk
1/3 cup arrowroot flour

In a mixing bowl, beat the egg whites until they are frothy peaks.

In a separate bowl, mix the egg yolks, syrup, cinnamon, milk and powder. Slowly add the egg whites. Add half of the coconut flour and mix slowly.

Slowly add the remaining coconut flour

Gently fold the mixtures together. As they start to combine, add the rest of the sifted flour. Fold until fully combined. Pour in to the bottom of a greased 9 x 13 pan.

Bake at 350 degrees for 15 to 18 minutes or until spongy. Dust with cinnamon and slice. Remove to plates and serve.

Coconut Porridge

In case your kids ever wanted to feel like Goldilocks, here is a porridge recipe you can have them try.

Ingredients:

¼ cup shredded coconut
¼ cup walnuts
¼ cup almonds
2 tbsp pumpkin seeds – still in shell
1 tbsp flaxseed
½ cup hot water
½ tbsp Honey

Using a food processor, grind the walnuts, almonds and seeds until they make a fine powder.

In a microwave safe bowl, boil the water. Stir in the honey and then the ground up mixture. Heat for an additional 30 seconds. Remove and allow to sit and thicken. Serve with more honey if desired.

Paleo Cereal

Some days it just feels good to have a big bowl of cereal and watch a few cartoons. This cereal recipe is Paleo friendly for the kids.

Ingredients:

½ apple, cored and diced
¼ cup sliced almonds
½ cup pitted, chopped dates
¼ cup shredded coconut
1/2 tsp cinnamon
1/8 tsp salt

Put all of the **Ingredients** in to a food processor and pulse gently. It will resemble granola. Pulse until the pieces are the adequate size for your child.

Serve with almond milk.

Banana Waffles

Waffles are a great way to fill up in the morning. This recipe gives them a banana flavor.

Ingredients:

1 medium banana
1 medium apple, peeled and cored
1 cup almond butter
2 eggs
1 tbsp arrowroot powder
1 tbsp vanilla
1/2 tsp baking soda

In a food processor, puree the apple and banana until they are almost smooth.

In a mixing bowl, whip the almond butter until it is fluffy. Pour in the banana mixture. Add the rest of the **Ingredients** and stir until combined.

Place the batter on a hot waffle iron and cook until browned on both sides.

Mini Frittatas

These mini frittatas can be customized to the **Ingredients** your child likes best.

Ingredients:

4 tablespoons fat
3 cloves of garlic, minced
½ medium onion, diced
½ pound of mushrooms, thinly sliced
8 large eggs
½ pound frozen spinach, thawed and squeezed dry
¼ cup coconut milk
2 tablespoons of coconut flour
5 ounces of Prosciutto
Salt and pepper to taste

Chop all of the veggies.

Heat the oil in a skillet and sauté the onions and the garlic. Add the mushrooms and cook until soft. Add salt and pepper to taste.

In a bowl, mix the eggs with the milk and flour. Add the rest of the **Ingredients**.

Line a muffin tin with the prosciutto. Pour the egg batter carefully in to the tins and bake at 375 degrees for 20 minutes.

Sausage & Eggs

This recipe is for sausage. It goes great with a batch of scrambled eggs.

Ingredients:

1 pound ground beef
2 tsp sage
½ tsp garlic powder
½ tsp mace - ground
½ tsp salt

In a bowl, mix the **Ingredients** together by hand. Form in to patties and place in the bottom of a hot skillet. Cook until browned on both sides. Serve hot with eggs or eat alone.

Chapter 2: Smoothie Recipes

In the morning, sometimes kids just don't want to eat a full meal. It might be too early, they might be in a hurry or they simply aren't that hungry. When that is the case, you can fill them up with a healthy smoothie. The smoothie recipes also work well for snacks after school when you still want them to eat a good dinner – just serve them a smaller portion.

Blueberry Smoothie

This blueberry smoothie recipe include chia seeds, a super antioxidant rich food that s just being discovered.

Ingredients:

2 frozen bananas
1 ½ cups fresh blueberries
4 Romaine lettuce leaves – washed and dried
2 cups almond milk
1 tbsp chia seeds

In a blender, combine all of the **Ingredients** until smooth. Serve chilled.

Berry Coconut Smoothie

This recipe uses fresh berries from the garden or farmer's market.

Ingredients:

1 cup fresh blueberries
1 cups fresh raspberries
2/3 cup shredded coconut
1 cup almond milk

Using a blender, pulse the berries. Add in the
remaining **Ingredients** and blend until smooth.
Makes two servings.

Tropical Smoothie

When you are looking for lots of vitamins, turn to this sweet smoothie.

Ingredients:

1 banana
1/2 apple
1 kiwi, peeled
1/2 cup frozen blueberries
1 cup orange juice
1/2 cup almond milk
1/2 cup plain yogurt
3 tbsp almond butter
2 tablespoons Aloe Vera Juice

In a blender, pulse the fruit until there are small chunks. Add the remaining **Ingredients** and blend until smooth.

Chocolate Smoothie

This chocolate smoothie can be served up after dinner and act like a dessert too.

Ingredients:
1 cup unsweetened almond milk
1 frozen banana
1 cup kale leaves – cleaned and dried
 1 tsp chia seeds
2 tbsp almond butter
1 tsp coconut oil
2 tsp cocoa powder

Add all of the **Ingredients** in to a blender. Pulse until they are coarsely combined. Then blend until smooth.

Pineapple Smoothie

When time is of the essence, serve this smoothie recipe to your kids.

Ingredients:

1/4 cup coconut milk
1 tbsp cacao nibs
¼ cup pineapple tidbits
3 oz water

In a blender, add the **Ingredients** and pulse until smooth.

Strawberry Smoothie

Strawberries are sweetest right when they are picked from the garden. Use this recipe to serve yours up.

Ingredients:

¾ cup of strawberries - hulled
¼ cup coconut milk
¼ cup crushed ice

In a blender, crush the ice. Add the remaining **Ingredients** and process until smooth.

Pumpkin Smoothie

If fall is in the air, how about making up this smoothie to really set the fall mood for the kids.

Ingredients:

1 cup pumpkin purée
1 cup coconut milk
1 frozen banana
2 tbsp almond butter
Cinnamon
ice cubes

Add the desired amount of ice cubes in a blender and pulse. Add the remaining **Ingredients** and blend until smooth.

Chapter 3: Brown Bag and Lunch Recipes

Lunch recipes that are Paleo friendly can be hard to come by, especially in a lunchroom setting at school. Therefore, finding items that work in the brown bag or even at home on the weekends can be tough. Following are a few great ideas to pack in a lunch – just make sure you have an ice pack to keep it cold and fresh.

Berry Yummy Salad

This salad is best when you can use fresh berries from the garden.

Ingredients:

Dressing
1/2 c. extra virgin olive oil
1/3 cup apple cider vinegar
1/4 cup honey
2 medium whole garlic cloves
1/4 tsp sea salt
1/4 tsp pepper
1/4 tsp dry mustard powder
1/4 tsp onion powder

1 cup toasted sunflower seeds, toasted

1 pound spinach leaves, trimmed and torn
1 pound butterhead lettuce, torn
1 bunch green onions, diced

1c fresh raspberries
1c fresh blueberries
1c fresh strawberries, sliced
1/3 cup chopped fresh dill weed

In a food processor, add all of the **Ingredients** for the dressing. Mix well and set aside.

In a large bowl, add the remaining **Ingredients** and toss. Drizzle the dressing over top. Store in individual sized bowls.

Broccoli Soup

This warm and creamy soup can be taken to school in a thermos to stay warm.

Ingredients:

2 cups bone broth
2 cups broccoli florets
1 avocado
½ tsp nutmeg

In a saucepan, place the florets. Cut and pit the avocado. Add the broth and bring to a simmer, stirring well. Reduce the heat and add the nutmeg. Cook for five minutes and then pour in to a blender and puree.

Chicken Wings

Is there a game on TV? Cook up a batch of wings and pretend like you are out at the restaurant with the kids watching it.

Ingredients:

3 pounds chicken wings
2 tbsp coconut oil
4 cloves garlic - diced
2 tbsp sesame oil
1 tbsp ground ginger
1 tsp fennel
1 tsp anise
½ cup coconut aminos
2 tbsp coconut vinegar
2 tbsp honey

1 tbsp fish sauce

In a saucepan, heat the coconut oil and add the ginger, garlic, anise and fennel for 3 minutes. Add the aminos, honey, vinegar and fish sauce and bring it to a boil. Simmer for one minute and then add the sesame oil and remove from the heat.

Place the wings in a bowl and pour the sauce over the top. Stir to coat and then place in the fridge to marinate overnight.

The next day, discard the marinade. Place the wings on a cookie sheet and bake at 375 degrees for 45 minutes or until cooked through.

Tuna Wraps

Place the tuna in a lettuce leaf and top with your favorite condiments.

Ingredients:

1 can tuna
Celery salt
Salt and pepper to taste
Romaine lettuce leaves

In a bowl, mix the **Ingredients** together. Add chopped onions, green peppers or green onions as desired. Scoop in to the center of a lettuce leaf and roll up from the bottom.

Ham & Avocado Roll Ups

These are simple and fast to prepare in the morning and send off to school.

Ingredients:

Ham slices
Avocado

Slice the cooked ham or use deli meat and lay the ham flat. Place thin avocado slice over the top. Roll from one end and secure with a toothpick.

Cucumber Sandwiches

These sandwiches are cute and can be eaten as a snack or sent in the lunch.

Ingredients:

1 cucumber
Salmon or tuna spread
Lettuce
Tomato slices

Peel the cucumber and cut in to circle slices. Spread 1 tsp of desired spread on top of one slice. Cover with tomato slice and then another cucumber piece. Secure with a toothpick.

Chicken Soup

You always need to have a good recipe for soup, especially when cold and flu season comes around.

Ingredients:

2-3 cups cooked chicken - cubed
½ cup carrots – diced
1 large onion - diced
3 fresh garlic cloves - minced
1 tsp sea salt
1 tsp pepper
Dash cayenne pepper
2 tbsp olive oil
2 tbsp coconut flour

In a large pot, sauté the oil and the vegetables until they are soft. Simmer for ten minutes. Add the chicken and the flour. Stir in 3 cups of water and bring the pot to a boil. Simmer on low for at least one hour. Pour in to t thermos to take to school or serve in a bowl.

Vegetable Soup

For the vegetarian or person who just wants a bunch of veggies, this soup recipe is delicious.

Ingredients:

1 pound of cubed chicken
1/2 cup diced red onions
1/2 cup diced green onions

1/2 cup green pepper diced
1 cup diced tomatoes
1 cup sliced zucchini
1 cup sliced carrots
1 cup cut celery
3 tablespoons diced fresh diced parsley
3 tablespoons diced fresh garlic
1 tsp salt
1 tsp grounded pepper
1 tablespoon olive oil
3 cups water

In a skillet, sauté the chicken until no longer pink.

In a saucepan, sauté the vegetables with the olive oil until they are soft.

In a pot, pour the contents of both skillets and combine with the water. Bring to a boil and then reduce the heat. Allow to simmer for one hour.

Chapter 4: Dinner Recipes

Dinner can be a time where the family sits down around the table and talks about their day. That might be in theory, if you have a busy calendar and multiple kids. Therefore, these fast and friendly recipes are easy to prepare and keep your family on the Paleo Diet.

Mini Meatballs

These meatballs can be eaten with a fork or a toothpick, depending on how much of a hurry you are in.

Ingredients:

2 tbsp coconut aminos
2 tsp fish sauce
1 tsp toasted sesame oil
1 pound ground pork
1 tbsp coconut flour
1 tbsp fresh grated ginger
1 bunch scallions, minced
coconut oil or lard, for greasing the pan

In a bowl, mix the aminos, oil, sauce, ginger and flour. Add the pork, scallions and mix with your hands until everything is combined. Form in to miniature meatballs and place on a greased cookie sheet. Bake at 425 degrees for twenty minutes. Serve with your favorite sauce.

Pasta

Everybody loves pasta! How about some zucchini pasta?

Ingredients:

4 large zucchini
2 tsp salt
1/3 cup bacon grease
2 large garlic cloves, crushed
¼ cup chopped fresh basil

Cut the zucchini in long, thin strips. Toss with the salt and leave in a bowl for one hour to soften. Rinse the salt of the zucchini and drain.

In a skillet, heat the grease and sauté the garlic until it is soft. Add the zucchini and cook for five minutes. Add the basil and stir until combined. Serve hot.

Turkey Roll Ups

These yummy sandwiches can be rolled up and eaten for lunch at home or served over a cold pack and taken to lunch.

Ingredients:

4 deli slices turkey
½ cucumber – sliced
½ tomato – sliced
Avocado – sliced

Spread the turkey out and lay flat on a counter. Arrange the tomato and cucumber slices and then top with avocado slice. Start at one end and roll up. Hold together with a toothpick if necessary. Eat right away or prepare for the lunch bag.

Paleo Pork Mein

When you feel like an Asian inspired entrée, turn to this pork recipe.

Ingredients:

2 tbsp coconut oil
1 lb thin sliced pork
1 small onion, wedged
1 5oz can water chestnuts - sliced
1 5oz can bamboo shoots – sliced
4 dried shiitake mushrooms – dried
8 baby bella mushrooms
3 baby bok choy
1 cup bone broth

1 tbsp coconut vinegar
1 pound Kelp Noodles
1 green onion

In a pot, soak the mushrooms for thirty minutes and then slice in to strips.

In a wok, add the oil when it is hot. Add the pork until it is browned. Add the vegetables, broth and vinegar. Cook for ten minutes or until the broth boils. Create a hole in the middle of the wok and add the kelp noodles. Simmer until they break up. Mix and serve. Garnish with chopped green onion.

Chicken Nuggets

These crispy chicken bites are the healthier alternative to nuggets that come breaded.

Ingredients:

1 pound boneless, skinless chicken cutlets
½ cup coconut flour
2 eggs

In a small pan, beat the egg. Place the coconut flour in another shallow dish.

Cut the chicken in to bite sized pieces and then dip in the egg to coat both sides. Dredge in the flour and then place in a greased baking dish. Cook at 350 degrees for 20 minutes or until the chicken juices run clear.

Baked Fish

Adding fish to the diet is a great way to keep it balanced.

Ingredients:

24 oz. cod fillets cut in to thick strips
1 1/2 cups of coconut flour
1 1/2 tsp of ginger powder
1/4 tsp of salt
2 cups coconut milk
1 cup finely shredded coconut
2 tbsp coconut oil

In a bowl, mix the flour, ginger powder and salt. In another bowl, add the coconut milk. In a third bowl, add the coconut.

Dip the fish pieces in the milk, then the flour, back in to the milk and then lastly in the coconut.

Place the pieces in a hot skillet and cook on both sides until golden brown.

Pork Chops

Pork chops are a great staple in the Paleo Diet. This easy recipe is great for a weekend dinner.

Ingredients:

2 lbs pork chops
2 tsp fennel seed
1 tsp salt
½ tsp cracked pepper

In a food processor, grind the fennel side in to a powder. Add salt and pepper to taste. Rub on both sides of the pork chops. Place the chops in to a 9 x 13 pan and place under the broiler. Cook for just 6 minutes on each side.

Spaghetti

This is a tried and true recipe that every kid loves to eat!

Ingredients:

2 lbs ground beef
1/4 tsp salt
1/4 cup fresh oregano, chopped

Combine the **Ingredients** until blended. Roll in to balls and place on a cookie sheet. Bake at 400 degrees for 15 minutes.

Ingredients (Spaghetti):

3 lbs summer squash
1 tbsp salt
12 cloves fresh garlic, minced
10 oz sliced mushrooms
3/4 cup fresh basil, chopped
meatballs

Cut the summer squash into long, thin pieces. Coat with salt and set aside for one hour.

Rinse and drain.

In a skillet, sauté the garlic and mushroom until they are soft. Add the squash noodles and stir for another 5 minutes. Add the basil and stir. Combine with the meatballs.

Tuna Packets

Instead of making tuna salad, how about cooking up a tuna steak?

Ingredients:

1/4 cup horseradish mustard
1/4 cup finely chopped parsley, divided
2 tbsp water
1/4 tsp pepper
2 baby bok choy, trimmed and quartered lengthwise
1 tablespoon extra-virgin olive oil
1 1/4 pounds tuna

In a small bowl, mix the mustard, 3 tbsp of parsley, water and pepper. Toss with the bok choy, oil and 2 tbsp of mustard sauce.

Cut four strips of aluminum foil. Place 2 bok choy quarters in the center of each one and then top with fish. Divide the sauce over the top and then salt and pepper to taste.

Fold the foil up and make sure the ends are pinched together.

Place on a cookie sheet and bake at 475 degrees for 15 minutes. Serve hot.

Shrimp Boil

This recipe will make you think you are down in the south, enjoying a traditional dish.

Ingredients:

4 lbs fresh whole shrimp
2 tbsp butter
5 large cloves chopped garlic
2 tbsp fresh parsley, chopped

Rinse the shrimp in a colander.

Using a large pot, heat the butter and garlic. Sauté until it is soft and add the shrimp. Cover with a lid and stir every two minutes. Toss with the parsley.

Tacos

Viva la Mexico! Enjoy this traditional menu entrée, without the shell.

Ingredients:

1 lb ground beef
½ large yellow onion, finely chopped
2 crushed garlic cloves
1 tbsp cooking fat
1 tbsp chili powder
1 tsp paprika
1½ tsp cumin
¼ tsp oregano
½ tsp salt
½ tsp ground pepper

In a skillet, brown the ground beef. Add the onion and garlic and cook until softened. Add the remaining spices and stir until combined. Allow the meat to simmer for 15 minutes.

Scoop in to lettuce leaves and roll up from the end to contain the meat.

BBQ Chicken

Everyone loves some good grilled chicken. This recipe uses a lot of spices to create a savory flavor.

Ingredients:

10 boneless, skinless chicken thighs

2 tsp paprika
2 tsp garlic powder
1 tsp ground cumin
1 tsp ground coriander
1 tsp salt
½ tsp fresh cracked pepper

In a bowl, mix all of the spices together. Rub on both sides of the chicken. Place it on a tray and take to the heated grill. Cook on medium high heat until both sides are firm and the chicken juices run dry.

Chapter 5: Snacks

One cannot leave by just meals alone! There are a lot of times where the kids need a healthy snack – while in the car on the way to practice. After school. Before bedtime. The amount of times when a snack needs to be had is limitless!

Apple Slices & Dip

This snack can be made by the children' themselves if they are old enough to handle a knife.

Ingredients:

1 apple
¼ cup nut butter of choice
Cut the apple in to wedges. Serve with prepared apple dip.

Kale Chips

Because sometimes you just need a little crunch! These take the place of potato chips as a snack or as a part of a brown bagged lunch.

Ingredients:

A few leaves of kale
1 tsp olive oil
1/9 tsp salt
Dash vinegar

Wash the kale and tear the leaves in to pieces. Dry and arrange over a cookie sheet. Sprinkle the oil over the top and bake in the oven at 350 degrees for 6 – 10 minutes. Season with salt and vinegar if desired. Cool and serve.

Cucumbers with Guacamole Dip

This dip can be taken to lunch on a cold pack or eaten after school.

Ingredients:

½ cup finely chopped fresh cilantro
2 ripe avocados
1 tbsp fresh lime juice
¼ tsp fresh cracked pepper
 1 cucumber

In a dish, scoop out the avocado and mash it. Stir in the remaining **Ingredients**.

Cut the cucumber in to spears and dip in the guacamole.

Apple Chips

Ingredients:

2 apples, cored
1/2 tsp cinnamon
1 lemon or lime

Slice the apples very thinly and place on a lined baking sheet. Sprinkle with the lemon juice and then the cinnamon. Bake at 225 degrees for 90 minutes. Remove from the oven and flip. Bake for an additional 90 minutes. Cool before storing in an airtight container.

Paleo Potato Skins

These Paleo potato skins are friendly because they are from sweet potatoes.

Ingredients:

1 tsp coconut oil
4 oz chopped mushrooms
½ cup chopped onions
4 oz bacon
2 medium sized sweet potatoes

Poke holes in to the potatoes and bake at 400 degrees for 45 minutes. Remove from the oven and cool.

In a skillet, sauté the onions and mushrooms in the oil until they are soft. Mix the bacon and set aside.

Cut the potatoes in half lengthwise and scoop out the insides. Place the skins with the opening on top. Fill with the stuffing mixture.. Bake at 425 degrees for 12 minutes.

Chapter 6: Dessert Recipes

No matter what diet you are following, you need to have some sweet treats! Your kids will love these sweet treats and might not even know they fall into a specific diet because they do taste just like "normal".

Blueberry Ice Cream

This recipe is best made in summer, when you can use fresh picked blueberries!

Ingredients:

2 cups fresh blueberries, divided
2 cans of coconut milk
1 tbsp plain gelatin
1/2 tsp vanilla
3/4 cup honey

Mix the berries with the milk, gelatin, vanilla, and honey. Stir until smooth and then pour in to the ice cream maker bowl. Pour the remaining blueberries over the top.

Follow the manufacturer's directions. Serve immediately or put in a smaller container and store in the freezer.

Brownies

This is a great recipe to use for an after school snack or in the lunch bag for school.

Ingredients:

1 egg
1 cup almond butter
3/4 cup cocoa powder
1 and 1/4 cup honey
2 teaspoons vanilla
1 teaspoon chocolate extract
1/2 teaspoon salt
1/2 teaspoon baking powder

In a bowl, stir the egg, vanilla, chocolate extract, salt, and baking powder.

In a saucepan, warm the honey and then add the cocoa powder. Stir until smooth and then pour in to the mixing bowl. Stir until combined and then pour in to a greased 8 x 8 pan. Bake for 45 minutes at 325 degrees.

Cool before slicing.

Chocolate Mousse

This makes a light end to a meal when you feel the need for a sweet cap.

Ingredients:

1 ripe avocado
1 banana cut in to chunks and then frozen
3 tbsp cacao powder

2 tbsp honey
Squeeze of lemon
Water as required
Pinch of sea salt

Using a blender, add the cacao powder and then the remaining **Ingredients**. Pulse until well blended and then continue until the mixture is smooth. Pour in to pudding cups to firm up and serve.

Zebra Bars

How about some chocolate with a little bit of butterscotch flavor to it?

Ingredients:

2 large overripe bananas
1/2 cup almond butter
3 eggs
1/4 cup coconut oil, melted
1 cup almond meal
3 Tbsp coconut flour
1/2 tsp baking soda
1/4 tsp salt
1/3 cup mini chocolate chips

Peel and mash the banana in to a medium bowl. Add the eggs, oil, butter, almond meal, flour, soda and salt. Stir until combined and then add the chocolate chips. Pour in to a greased 9 x 13 pan. Bake at 350 degrees for 18 minutes. Cool before cutting in to squares.

Coconut Popsicles

This frozen treat makes a great snack on a hot summer day.

Ingredients:

2 cups shredded unsweetened coconut, divided
1 banana, mashed
1/4 cup melted coconut butter
1/4 cup coconut milk
Zest from 1 lime
Pinch sea salt

On a baking sheet, spread out 1 cup of coconut and toast in the oven at 300 degrees for 15 minutes. Stir every 5 minutes. Remove and set aside.

In a mixing bowl, mash the banana, coconut butter, milk, zest and salt. Add the toasted coconut and combine. Press the mixture in to the cups of a muffin tin and freeze. Stick a wooden stick in before freezing.

Freeze overnight before serving.

Paleo Rocky Road Bars

When you feel like you need a reward, this recipe does the trick!

Ingredients:

1/2 cup maple syrup
1/3 cup palm shortening

2 eggs
2 1/2 cups almond flour
1 tsp baking soda
1/2 tsp salt
1/4 cup cacao ground nibs
1/2 cup dark chocolate chips
1/2 cup marshmallows, diced to 1/2″ square
1/2 cup chopped walnuts

In a bowl, blend the palm shortening and maple syrup. Beat in the eggs.

In a separate bowl, mix the flour, soda and salt. Add the cacao and the remaining dry **Ingredients**. Combine with the syrup and stir. Fold in the chocolate chips, nuts and marshmallows. Press in to a greased 9 x 9 pan. Bake for 25 minutes at 350 degrees. Cool before slicing in to squares and serving.

Blueberry Cookies

The fresh blueberries make this treat good for anytime of the day, not just after school.

Ingredients:

1 cup sunflower seeds
1/2 cup cashews
1/2 cup walnuts
1/3 cup palm shortening
1/4 cup granulated maple sugar
1/2 tsp salt
1 egg
zest and juice of 1 lemon (about 2 tablespoons)
2 tbsp tapioca flour
1 tsp baking soda
1/2 tsp cream of tartar
1 cup fresh blueberries

In a food processor, grind the sunflower seeds, cashews and walnuts.

In another bowl, blend the palm shortening, sugar, egg and lemon juice and zest. Stir in the flour, tapioca flour, soda and cream of tartar. Add to the processed **Ingredients** and stir just until combined. Fold in the blueberries.

Drop by teaspoons on to a cookie sheet. Bake for 14 minutes at 350 degrees. Set on a wire rack to cool.

Cut Out Cookies

These cookies aren't just for Christmas; they can be made any time of the year in to a fun shape.

Ingredients:

1/3 cup extra virgin coconut oil
4 oz unsweetened chocolate
½ cup honey
4 eggs
1 tbsp vanilla
1 cup coconut flour

In a microwave safe bowl, melt the oil and chocolate on medium. Stir and add the honey, vanilla and eggs. Add the flour.

Store in the refrigerator for two hours to chill.

Roll the dough out on a covered surface until it is ¼" thick. Cut with shapes and place on a cookie sheet. Bake for 12 minutes. Remove to a wire rack to cool.

Chocolate Clusters

When you want a rich treat, these clusters will do the trick. And the best part is you don't need to feel guilty about giving them to your kids because they are Paleo friendly.

Ingredients:

1 cup plus 3 tablespoons melted dark chocolate
1 1/2 cups whole almonds
Handful of coconut shavings

In a microwave safe bowl, melt the chocolate.

Lay out two sheets of waxed paper. Arrange thee almonds together in a cluster evenly over the sheet. Pour a tablespoon of melted chocolate over the dust. Dust with coconut shavings.

Made in the USA
Middletown, DE
19 March 2015